HANDS TOGETHER EYES CLOSED

IVAN E. STREET

Hands together eyes closed

ST PAULS

Cover and illustrations by Sarah John

ST PAULS
Middlegreen, Slough SL3 6BT, United Kingdom
Moyglare Road, Maynooth, Co. Kildare, Ireland

© ST PAULS 1993

ISBN 085439 459 1

Printed by The Guernsey Press Co., Guernsey, C.I.

ST PAULS is an activity of the priests and brothers of the Society of St Paul who proclaim the Gospel through the media of social communication

Contents

1. Family and Friends — 7
2. Animals — 17
3. Weather — 25
4. Sand and Sea — 33
5. Food — 41
6. Creation — 49
7. Caring People — 59
8. Transport — 69
9. Leisure — 77
10. School — 87

1
Family and Friends

Dear Jesus,

Bless all our family.
There are so many in it.
Some are young, some are old.
Take care of them all please.
Feed them, clothe them.
Shelter them, love them.
May they remember you also.
Amen.

Dear Jesus,

Look after our friends.
Sometimes we are caring,
Sometimes we are selfish,
Sometimes we all fall out,
Sometimes we make up again.
Remind us to treat our friends
As we like to be treated
   ourselves.
Amen.

Dear Jesus,

Take care of our parents.
They take care of us.
Let our parents be happy,
They make us happy too.
Love our parents a lot.
They love us always.
Watch over our parents today.
They watch us eagerly.
May we do our best for them.
They do their best for us.
Amen.

Dear Jesus,

Thank you for all our friends.
They mean so much to us.
They play and share and care
    with us.
Let us remember those who find
    it difficult to make friends.
Help us to make the first move
    to say Hello to them.
Amen.

Dear Jesus,

What a lot of people in our family!
Grandmothers and Grandfathers.
Mums and Dads.
Brothers and Sisters.
Nieces and Nephews.
Aunts and Uncles.
What a lot of people to love.
We know that your arms stretch wide.
Thank you, Lord.
Amen.

Dear Jesus,

Some of our friends live near to us.
Some of our friends live far away.
Some of our friends are girls.
Some of our friends are boys.
Some of our friends are tall.
Some of our friends are small.
Some of our friends are sad.
Some of our friends are happy.
All of our friends are precious.
All of our friends are special.
Bless them all.
Amen.

2
Animals

Dear Jesus,

How the fish swim around in their home!
It's lovely to see the bubbles rising.
The fish seem to stare and are easily frightened.
They trust us to give them their food though.
May we be relied upon to look after them for you.
Amen.

Dear Jesus,

How big cows are!
Full of pattern, full of colour.
How good that they give us milk.
How marvellous that it makes
   cream, yoghurt and cheese.
Thank you for cows, bulls and
   calves.
Amen.

Dear Jesus,

We are sure that you would like our cats.
You would stroke them, fuss them, want to pick them up.
Some of the time they are playful.
The rest of the time they are sleepy.
Thank you for letting them belong to us.
Amen.

Dear Jesus,

Dogs run, dogs play.
Dogs jump, dogs bark.
Dogs are patient, dogs are friendly.
Dogs are loyal, dogs are great.
We are pleased and glad that you have given us dogs.
May we teach them correct and treat them well.
Amen.

Dear Jesus,

Thank you for all animals.
Birds, beast, insects and fish.
May we be kind and caring at all times to them.
May we help to provide homes and food for them.
May we never be unkind and cruel to them.
Amen.

Dear Jesus,

How super to see the variety of animals!
Tall ones, small ones, big ones, little ones.
Black ones, white ones, coloured ones, patterned ones.
Some walking, some running, some flying, some swimming.
Some angry, some gentle, some rough, some smooth.
All needing shelter and food.
Remind us of our responsibilities and what we have to do in your name.
Amen.

3
Weather

Dear Jesus,

How lovely to walk in puddles!
How great to let water trickle
   through your fingers!
How grand to wear wellingtons
   and macs!
Thank you for the gentle
   showers, the falling rain,
And running water.
It brings life itself.
Amen.

Dear Jesus,

Gliding leaves and bowing trees.
Floating scrap and bending flowers.
The wind shapes and moves all
   things.
We cannot see wind.
Only measure the effect that it has.
Its the same with you, Lord.
Amen.

Dear Jesus,

Sunshine makes us feel good.
Sunshine makes us feel warm.
Sunshine makes the plants grow.
Sunshine lights all around us.
Sunshine is so necessary for all
 your children.
May we feel good, warm and
 able to grow.
Let our light shine around us,
So that people may see a little of
 you, Lord.
Amen.

Dear Jesus,

Sometimes the weather is too
  strong for us.
The wind is rough.
The rain is heavy.
The sun is strong.
Thank you for protection against
  the elements.
Our clothes.
Our umbrellas.
Our dark glasses.
These all help our need.
Amen.

Dear Jesus,

How silently the snowflakes fall!
Overnight there is a thick white carpet.
What fantastic games we can play!
We can build. We can sledge.
Help us to realise what a wonderful sight and picture it all makes.
Amen.

Dear Jesus,

Thank you for all the changing scenes of life.
The white of snow.
The dark of clouds.
The warmth of sun.
The cold of ice.
The thick damp fog.
The clear blue sky.
Help us to cope with the weather.
Help us to look in wonder.
Help us to marvel at the changing seasons.
Amen.

4
Sand and Sea

Dear Jesus,

My! How the sea roars over the pebbles.
Then the waves lap the shore.
My! How the sea leaps up high.
Then it plunges low with a quick roll.
My! How beautiful the sea is.
Then so cruel as it beats against the sea wall.
You rule the mighty oceans, Lord.
Amen.

Dear Jesus,

We love to see the ships and boats and yachts.
With their engines, and oars, and sails.
Lovely to see them riding and tossing and floating.
How small they all look on the great sea!
Bless all the people who use them for work and play.
Please keep them safe and out of danger.
Amen.

Dear Jesus,

Thank you for the super sand on
   which we walk.
Thank you for the super sand in
   which we play.
Thank you for the super sand
   which forms our beaches.
Lots of exercise.
Lots of fun.
Lots of beauty.
Amen.

Dear Jesus,

How marvellous to stare at the cliffs!
They are so huge and rugged.
They are so majestic and strong.
Thank you for the pathways down to the beach.
Thank you for the wonderful wildflowers strewn about.
Thank you for the grandeur of Nature.
Amen.

Dear Jesus,

We know that you loved the sea.
We know that you had a boat.
We know that your friends were
 fishermen.
Going on our holidays reminds
 us of some of the things
 that you did.
May the seaside bring happy
 memories back to us, and
may we feel better for having
 been there.
Amen.

Dear Jesus,

Thank you for the gulls in flight.
Thank you for the golden sands.
Thank you for the sloping cliffs.
Thank you for the colourful seaweed.
Thank you for the smooth pebbles.
Thank you for the clear skies.
Thank you for the tossing sea.
Thank you for the lapping waves.
Thank you for the magic of holidays.
Amen.

5
Food

Dear Jesus,

We are grateful for grain.
Oats, barley, rye and wheat.
So small a seed gives us so much.
The cakes we eat, the bread we chew.
The biscuits we crunch, the cereal we relish.
We thank you for our Daily Bread.
And ask that you provide for all people.
Amen.

Dear Jesus,

Mealtimes are always welcome.
Looking forward to them is fun.
Many times we are surprised.
Rarely are we ever left empty.
Food gives us the energy to play.
Let us remember those people
 who provide it for us.
Amen.

Dear Jesus,

All of us like some fruit.
Apples, pears, peaches, plums.
Fruit is full of vitamins.
And therefore good for us.
Thank you for the trees and
  bushes,
  which yield our choice.
Thank you for the people and
  countries,
  which supply our need.
Amen.

Dear Jesus,

Eating out is really good.
Birthdays, Special Days,
 Celebrations.
It's lovely to eat with friends.
Lunch or tea or dinner.
How fortunate we are to have
 choice!
So many people in our world
 have none.
May we count our blessings
 when we have our food
 prepared for us.
Let us be thankful.
Amen.

Dear Jesus,

Bless the farmers working their land.
Bless the workers gathering the crops.
How important it is that we have vegetables!
Potatoes, carrots, parsnips, peas.
All of these help us to grow.
As we eat, Lord, let us remember
All the work necessary to provide our food.
Amen.

Dear Jesus,

Thank you for the simple potato.
There is so much to do with it.
Chipped and roasted, baked and boiled.
They give so much nourishment each time.
Thank you for the fields in which they grow.
Thank you for the farmers who harvest them.
A simple shape, a simple size.
A simple cooking, a simple taste.
So much goodness for all to enjoy.
Amen.

6
Creation

Dear Jesus,

How big the Universe is!
How large the Planets are!
How vast are the Continents!
How great are the Oceans!
How small we are, Lord!
Yet, you know all of us.
That makes us feel good.
Amen.

Dear Jesus,

Light and Dark.
Day and Night.
Water and Land.
Sea and Earth.
In the beginning God created the Heavens and the Earth.
Thank you for making it so well ordered and good.
May we play our part in keeping it well.
Amen.

Dear Jesus,

Hedgerows and berries.
Ditches and flowers.
Heaths and grasses.
Mountains and plants
All were made to order and in
 turn.
Let us take care
 of our heritage.
Let us keep it safe and secure.
Lord, may we be its keeper.
Amen.

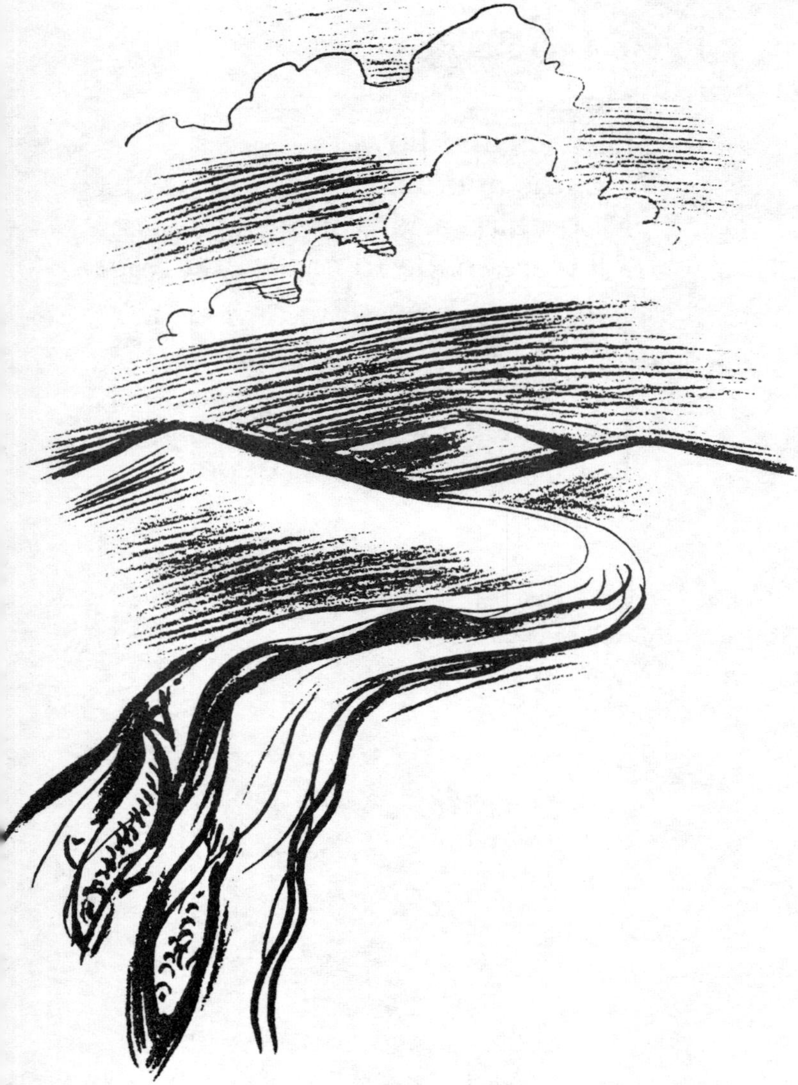

Dear Jesus,

Streams and Rivers and Seas.
Orchards and Woods and
 Forests.
Peaks and Hills and Mountains.
Lowlands and Valleys and Plains.
All these were created for us to
 enjoy.
May we treat them properly and
 value them.
How great you are, Lord.
Amen.

Dear Jesus,

Thank you for the open sky.
In the day so very clear.
Blue with moving clouds.
At the night so very dark.
Alive with shooting stars.
How good we feel knowing of
 your creative hand!
How secure we feel knowing of
 your balanced Universe!
Amen.

Dear Jesus,

Thank you for the variety of flowers.
Colours, size, and pattern.
Thank you for the selection of trees.
Colour, size, and pattern.
Thank you for the choice of plants.
Colour, size, and pattern.
Flowers, trees, and plants.
All were made to your command, Lord.
All were made for our pleasure and delight.
Amen.

7
Caring People

Dear Jesus,

Tall and uniformed.
Straight and smart.
Our Police friends are.
Correct and fair.
Right and brave.
Patrolling where we live.
May we listen and learn and
 respect them.
They have a job to do.
We have to live by the rules and
 laws of the Land.
Amen.

Dear Jesus,

Occasionally we may be ill.
Sometimes we don't feel well.
Briefly we are off colour.
If necessary we have to go to
 Hospital.
Bless the Doctors and Nurses
 who attend to our needs.
Give them knowledge and
 strength with ability to cope
With all the tasks that they are
 called upon to do.
Amen.

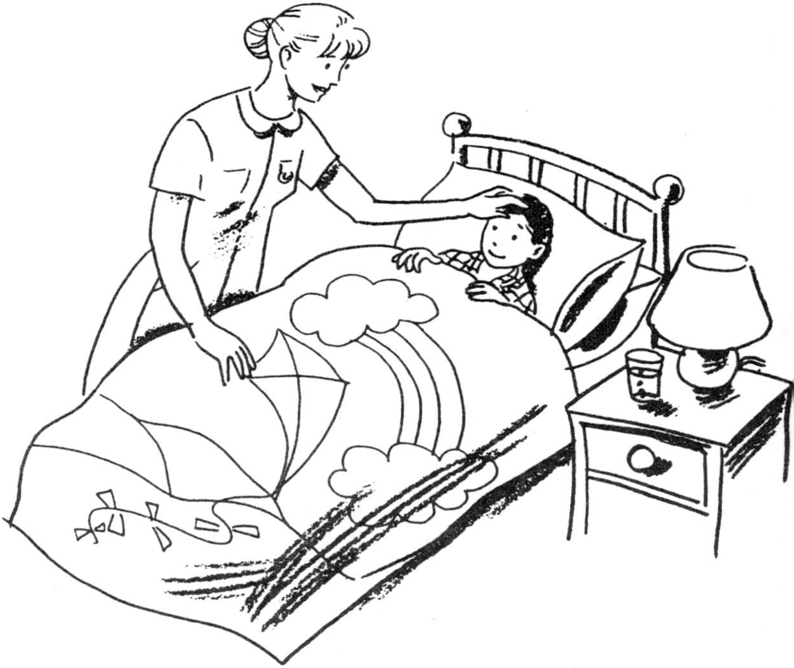

St David was teacher so today lets us pray for the teachers we know.

Dear Jesus,

We expect Teachers to know a lot of things.
We expect Teachers to read a number of books.
We expect Teachers to be very patient.
We expect Teachers to have a sense of humour.
We expect Teachers to work amongst us.
We know that Teachers will be caring.
~~May our expectations all be realised.~~
~~Amen.~~ and we pray for our own teachers - giving thanks for all they do for us. We pray for Mr Webster, Mrs Seabrook, Mrs Mosely and Mrs Pitton.
Look after them Jesus and give them the strength they need for the work they have to do.
Amen.

Dear Jesus,

Books are like children.
They need treating with care.
There are thousands of books in our Library.
Books are like doors.
They need opening and closing.
There are thousands of pages to read.
Thank you for all the people that work in Libraries.
They work hard. They are quiet.
They help us. They answer questions.
Amen.

Dear Jesus,

Our Leisure Centre is tremendous.
What a lot of activities we can do!
Skip, run, jump, swim and play.
Our Leisure Centre is great.
What a lot of people we can meet!
Relatives, neighbours, friends.
Our Leisure Centre is super.
A fine collection of kind people.
Attendants, Supervisors, Teachers, Cleaners.
Thank you for all the interesting folks.
Amen.

Dear Jesus,

Many times we go into shops.
There are many different ones in Town.
People work hard serving others.
Standing up all day.
Answering questions.
Giving attention.
Wrapping things up.
Give all shop assistants enthusiasm, cheerfulness and patience.
Amen.

8
Transport

Dear Jesus,

No where is really far now.
The motor car eats roads up.
No distance ever takes long.
The motor car makes miles
   vanish.
We love to hear the engine tick.
The hedgerows swish by fast,
Thank you for all the cars,
And the convenience that they
   give.
Amen.

Dear Jesus,

Is your journey necessary?
Is your journey necessary?
Yes, it is. Yes, it is.
Faster we go. Faster we go.
End in sight. End in sight.
What a pleasure to travel!
What a delight to journey!
Trains give comfort and warmth
and speed.
Lord, thank you for all their
power.
Amen.

Dear Jesus,

Just like a bird it is, Lord.
With wings outstretched.
What a lovely shape,
A smooth streamlined design!
It will take us over the water.
A journey through the clouds.
Higher and higher will it climb.
Lower and lower until it lands.
We marvel at the aeroplane.
Amen.

Dear Jesus,

Round and round the pedals go.
Thank you for strength in our legs.
Miles and miles turn the wheels.
Using our energy all up.
The bicycle was a present to us,
 Lord.
It makes us take great care.
Please make us ever mindful of all
 the danger around.
We are grateful to be able to travel.
Amen.

Dear Jesus,

Roads, Streets, Avenues,
Crescents.
Lanes, Motorways, Boulevards,
Drives.
All of these traffic drives upon.
We thank you, Lord, that we are able
To get from one place to another easily.
May we take care when playing near busy areas.
Amen.

Dear Jesus,

We love the interest of buses.
Their size and colour excite us.
Thank you for making it easy to travel.
It is good to watch the countryside go by.
It's great to sit and feel the speed.
Thank you for making it fun to travel.
Thank you for all who drive for us.
Thank you for the people who make the buses.
Amen.

9
Leisure

Dear Jesus,

Thank you for all the free time that we have.
May we use it well.
Let us walk and enjoy the countryside.
The wildflowers, the variety of plants.
Let us come back refreshed.
Feeling good and free.
Thank you for all our leisure time.
Amen.

Dear Jesus,

There are so many games to play.
Football, Cricket, Netball, Tennis.
There is so much to do, Lord.
Never enough time to do it in.
Whenever and whatever we play,
May we be good losers as well as victorious winners.
The game is the all important thing.
Remember there is always tomorrow.
Amen.

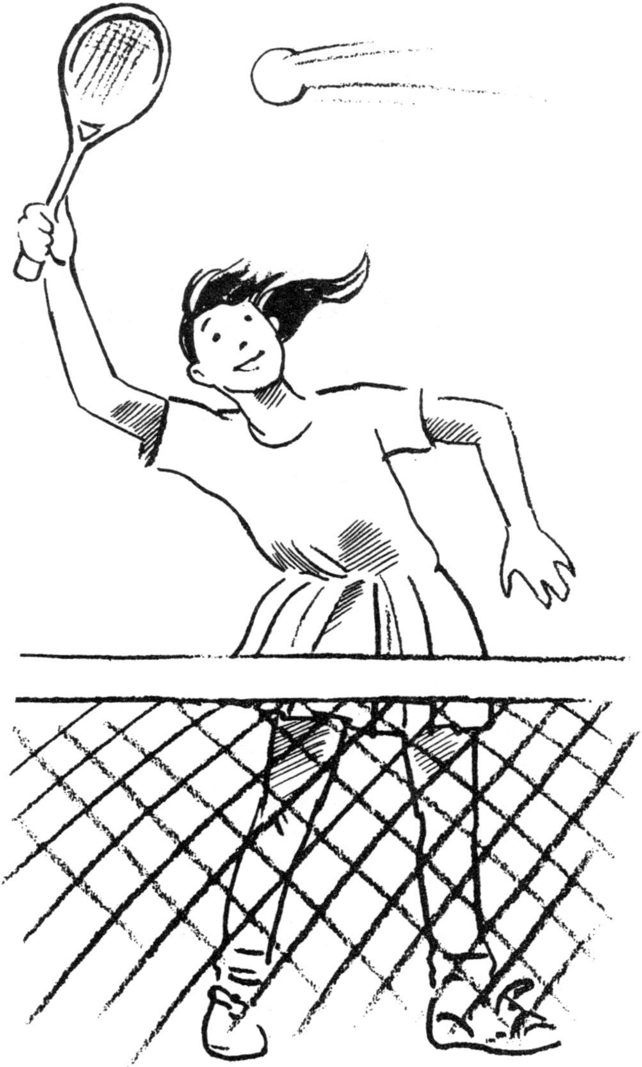

Dear Jesus,

May we never be bored.
Lord, there is so much to do.
The Park with open spaces,
Its borders filled with flowers.
The fields with dancing grass.
Its paths so narrow, but fun.
May we enjoy the fine fresh air.
Fill our lungs with clean air.
Thank you for all in Nature.
Amen.

Dear Jesus,

Encourage us to choose carefully,
What we do with our spare time.
Help us to think about what
 Organisations to join.
May we serve you, and by that
 serve other people too.
Take our time and our talents
 and turn them to good use in
 your name.
Amen.

Dear Jesus,

We get a lot of pleasure from swimming.
Good exercise, great fun,
Lovely diving, natural strokes.
It is a super feeling gliding through the water.
It is a real treat jumping in from the side.
Thank you for the ability to swim.
May we pass it on to someone else.
Amen.

Dear Jesus,

How fortunate we are to play music!
Thank you for all the instruments of
Band and Orchestra.
Let us be ever ready to listen to all kinds of music.
Let us appreciate what is played for us.
May we practise to become better players.
May we use our gifts to please others.
Amen.

10
School

Dear Jesus,

Bless our School.
May it be a place of learning.
Let it be a happy place.
Give us respect for the Staff,
And respect for one another.
May our learning be exciting,
Make all of us do our best.
At all times may we pay
   attention.
Bless our School.
Amen.

Dear Jesus,

We start a new day.
We start a clean sheet.
Let us be careful what we do.
We start a new book.
We start a clear page.
Let us think what we are doing.
Yesterday has gone,
Tomorrow is to be.
Today we do our best.
Amen.

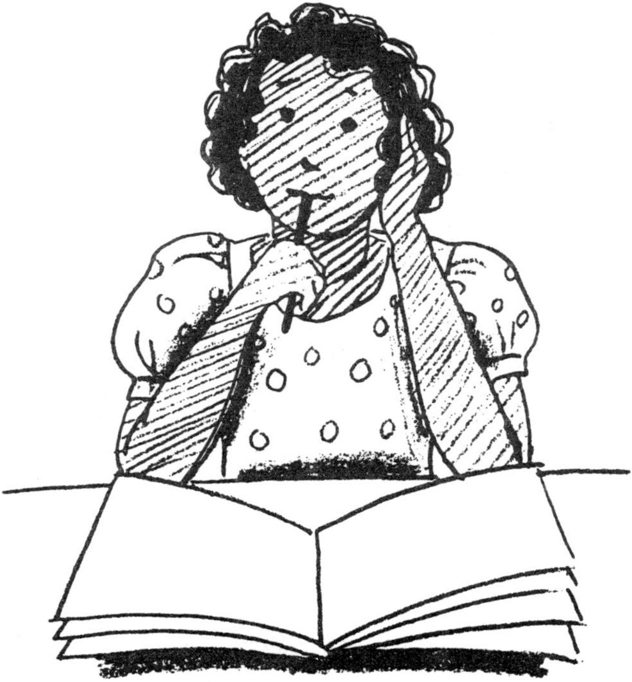

Dear Jesus,

"If a job's worth doing,
It's worth doing well."
May that be our motto.
Give us a desire to do our best,
Whatever the job, whatever the task.
May we concentrate awhile.
May we work really hard.
May we get satisfaction from our lessons.
Help us, Lord, we pray,
in all that we do.
Amen.

Dear Jesus,

All together we now meet.
Staff and pupils combine.
Lord, we ask your blessing.
Guide us, guard us,
Keep us, protect us.
Grant your peace upon us now.
May we do a good deed today.
May we be kind to some one.
In your name hear our prayer.
Amen.

Dear Jesus,

Time waits for no man.
The day has now gone.
We close our books awhile.
We put our things away.
Thank you for our time together.
Thank you for our fellowship
  here.
Tomorrow is a new day,
We look forward to that.
Amen.

Dear Jesus,

What a wonderful day it's been.
Enjoyment has been ours.
Friendship has been here.
Happiness has thrived.
Satisfaction has been achieved.
Learning has taken place.
Bless our class.
Bless our School.
May we remember our School
   days with joy and love.
Amen.